MW00910198

THE COMIC BOOK BIBLE

FROM ADAM TO JACOB

Published by Scandinavia Publishing House 2011

Scandinavia Publishing House, Drejervej 15,3, DK-2400 Copenhagen, NV, Denmark

Tel. (45) 3531 0330   E-mail: info@scanpublishing.dk   Web: www.scanpublishing.dk

Concept by Jose Perez Montero

Text copyright © Ben Alex

Illustrations copyright © Jose Perez Montero

Design by Ben Alex

Printed in China

Hardcover ISBN 9788772472003

Softcover ISBN 9788772471990

All rights reserved

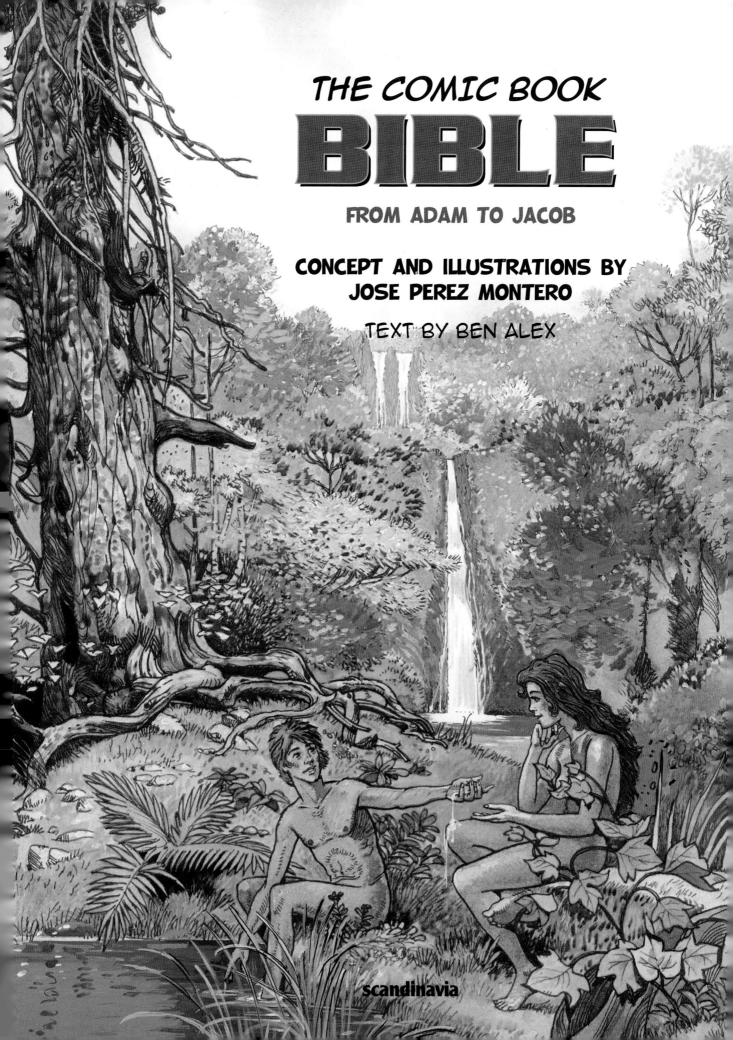

BEFORE GOD CREATED THE UNIVERSE AND THE EARTH, THERE WAS ONLY DARKNESS AND SILENCE...

THE CREATION OF THE WORLD Genesis 1:1-25

THEN GOD SPOKE AND CREATED THE SKIES AND THE EARTH. BUT ALL WAS STILL DARK AND EMPTY.

THEN GOD SAID, "LET THERE BE LIGHT!"

AND HE SEPARATED THE LIGHT FROM DARKNESS.

GOD CALLED THE LIGHT DAY, AND THE DARKNESS NIGHT.

THEN GOD CREATED OCEANS AND LAND.

THE OCEANS HE FILLED WITH FISH AND ALL THE CREATURES THAT LIVE IN WATER.

THE LAND HE FILLED WITH PLANTS AND COUNTLESS BIRDS AND ANIMALS. GOD SAW THAT EVERYTHING WAS GOOD.

GOD SAID, "LET US MAKE MAN
IN OUR OWN IMAGE AND LIKENESS.
HE WILL TAKE CARE OF ALL
THE LIVING THINGS THAT ARE CREATED."

SO GOD FIRST CREATED
MAN FROM DUST AND
GAVE HIM LIFE.

HE NAMED MAN ADAM AND PUT
HIM IN THE GARDEN OF EDEN.

GOD TOLD ADAM TO GIVE NAMES TO
ALL THE CREATURES IN THE GARDEN.
ADAM DID WHAT GOD ASKED, AND
THE ANIMALS BECAME HIS FRIENDS.

ADAM AND EVE IN THE GARDEN OF EDEN Genesis 1:1-26; 2:1-25

BUT SOMETHING WAS STILL MISSING.

GOD SAW THAT ADAM WAS LONELY. "IT'S NOT GOOD FOR MAN TO BE ALONE," HE SAID.

WHILE ADAM WAS ASLEEP, GOD TOOK ONE OF HIS RIBS AND FORMED A PARTNER, A WOMAN. HE NAMED HER EVE.

WHEN ADAM WOKE UP, HE SAW A BEAUTIFUL WOMAN AT HIS SIDE.

EVE!

WE ARE ALIKE!

ADAM!

ADAM AND EVE LIVED TOGETHER IN THE GARDEN. THEY WERE HAPPY AND NAKED AND WERE NOT ASHAMED.

AFTER GOD HAD CREATED THE WORLD, HE RESTED. AND HE SAW THAT ALL WAS VERY GOOD.

BUT THE SERPENT WAS A CRAFTY CREATURE.

DID GOD REALLY SAY YOU MUST NOT EAT FROM THE TREES?

NO, ONLY THE TREE OF KNOWLEDGE. IF WE EAT FROM THAT TREE, WE WILL DIE.

WELL, GOD SAID THAT BECAUSE HE IS AFRAID YOU WILL BE AS WISE AS HE IS!

ONE LITTLE BITE CAN'T HURT.

ADAM ALSO TOOK A BITE...

NO!

ADAM AND EVE HAD DISOBEYED GOD'S COMMAND NOT TO EAT OF THE FORBIDDEN TREE OF GOOD AND EVIL. THIS PUT A TERRIBLE END TO THEIR HAPPINESS.

THEY WERE HORRIFIED AND EMBARRASSED WHEN THEY SAW EACH OTHER NAKED.

GASP!

COME, LET'S HIDE.

COULD THEY HIDE FROM GOD? NO, THAT'S IMPOSSIBLE. GOD KNOWS US BETTER THAN WE KNOW OURSELVES.

THE FALL Genesis 3:1-24

LATER THAT AFTERNOON GOD WAS LOOKING FOR ADAM AND EVE...

ADAM, WHERE ARE YOU?

I HEARD YOU WALKING IN THE GARDEN, AND I HID BECAUSE I WAS NAKED.

WHO TOLD YOU THAT YOU WERE NAKED?

GOD KNEW THAT ADAM AND EVE HAD EATEN FROM THE TREE OF KNOWLEDGE ALTHOUGH HE HAD TOLD THEM NOT TO.

THE WOMAN YOU GAVE ME TOLD ME TO EAT IT!

THE SERPENT SAID I COULD!

CURSED ARE YOU! MAN SHALL CRUSH YOUR HEAD, AND YOU WILL STRIKE HIS HEEL.

CAIN AND ABEL Genesis 4:1-16

EVE GAVE BIRTH TO A THIRD SON AND NAMED HIM SETH.

CAIN'S WIFE ALSO GAVE BIRTH TO A SON.

THEIR SONS AND DAUGHTERS ALSO HAD CHILDREN, AND OVER TIME THE POPULATION OF THE EARTH GREW. PEOPLE WERE DIVIDED INTO NATIONS AND RACES,

BUT BECAUSE OF ADAM AND EVE'S DISOBEDIENCE, EVIL SPREAD AMONG MEN.

PEOPLE EVEN BEGAN TO KILL ONE ANOTHER JUST LIKE CAIN HAD KILLED HIS BROTHER ABEL.

GOD SAW THIS EVIL AND REGRETTED THAT HE HAD MADE MANKIND.

SO HE DECIDED TO DESTROY ALL HE HAD ONCE CREATED IN LOVE.

HOWEVER, THERE WAS STILL ONE GOOD AND HONEST MAN LEFT ON EARTH.

NOAH, I'M GOING TO DESTROY THE WORLD,

BUT I WILL SPARE YOU AND YOUR FAMILY.

GOD TOLD NOAH AND HIS THREE SONS TO BUILD AN ARK.

I WILL MAKE A COVENANT WITH YOU.

WHATEVER YOU SAY, LORD.

GOD TOLD NOAH TO BRING HIS FAMILY AND ONE PAIR OF EVERY LIVING THING INTO THE ARK.

NOAH AND THE GREAT FLOOD Genesis 6:5-8:12

NOAH DIDN'T HAVE TO GO OUT AND CATCH ALL THOSE ANIMALS. THEY CAME BY THEMSELVES, AND NOAH LET THEM INTO THE ARK.

AS SOON AS EVERYONE'S INSIDE, CLOSE THE DOOR AND WAIT.

I WILL LET IT RAIN FOR FORTY DAYS AND FORTY NIGHTS. EVERY LIVING THING ON EARTH WILL DIE.

COME ON, HURRY UP!

FINALLY, EVERYONE WAS SAFELY INSIDE THE ARK.

SLAM!

SCREECH

SOON AFTER, THEY HEARD RAIN TAPPING ON THE ROOF.

DON'T WORRY, SONS. GOD KNOWS WHAT HE'S DOING.

MANY DAYS PASSED, AND THE RAIN WENT ON AND ON. BUT NOAH AND HIS FAMILY WERE SAFE IN THE ARK.

ONE DAY, THEY HEARD A RUMBLE, THEN FELT A JOLT. SUDDENLY, THE ARK ROSE AND WAS AFLOAT.

IT RAINED FOR FORTY DAYS AND FORTY NIGHTS, JUST AS GOD HAD TOLD NOAH.

THE WATER FROM BELOW ALSO KEPT RISING, BUT THE ARK ROSE AND FLOATED ON THE SURFACE. BUT BELOW, EVERY LIVING THING ON EARTH DIED IN THE FLOOD.

A NEW WORLD   Genesis 8:13-9-29

NOAH PLANTED A VINEYARD, AND HIS SONS SHEM, HAM AND JAPHETH BECAME FARMERS. FROM THEM THE WHOLE EARTH WAS POPULATED.

TIME PASSED. NEW GENERATIONS WERE BORN. NOAH'S DESCENDANTS MOVED FROM THE EAST TO THE PLAINS OF SHINAR. THEY ALL SPOKE THE SAME LANGUAGE.

AMONG THEM WERE SOME INDUSTRIOUS MEN. THEY CAME UP WITH A PLAN.

LET'S GET TOGETHER AND BUILD A GREAT CITY!

GREAT! A FORTIFIED, INVINCIBLE CITY!

YEAH! WITH A TALL TOWER. THIS WILL SHOW EVERYONE HOW GREAT WE ARE. WE'LL BECOME WORLD FAMOUS!

ALAS! THEY HAD FORGOTTEN ABOUT GOD. INSTEAD OF WORSHIPING HIM, THEY WANTED TO CREATE A NAME FOR THEMSELVES.

GOD WAS VERY SAD. HE SAW THAT ONCE AGAIN MANKIND WAS HEADING FOR A DISASTER.

WE'LL BUILD A TOWER THAT REACHES THE SKIES.

TALLER THAN THAT. A TOWER THAT REACHES HEAVEN!

27TH FLOOR IS ALMOST DONE!

SO THEY CHANGED THEIR PLANS. THEY CUT STONES AND MADE BRICKS AND MORTAR. THE TOWER GREW HIGHER AND HIGHER.

THE TOWER OF BABEL Genesis 11:1-9

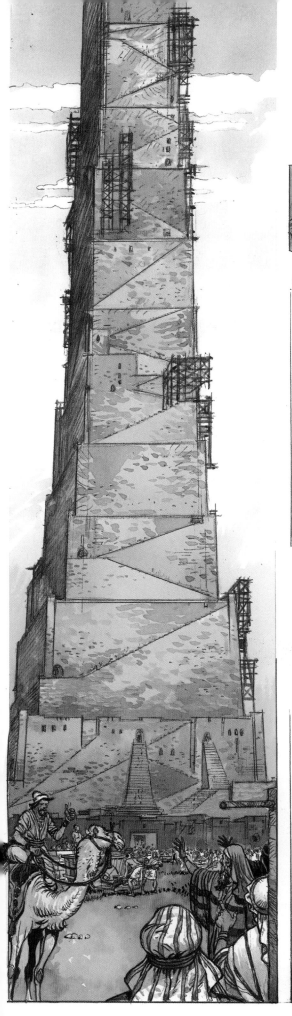

FINALLY GOD CAME DOWN TO TAKE A LOOK. "THERE'S NO LIMIT," HE SAID, "TO WHAT PEOPLE CAN ACCOMPLISH WHEN THEY WORK TOGETHER AS ONE. THIS IS ONLY THE FIRST STEP. WHO KNOWS WHAT THEY WILL COME UP WITH NEXT?"

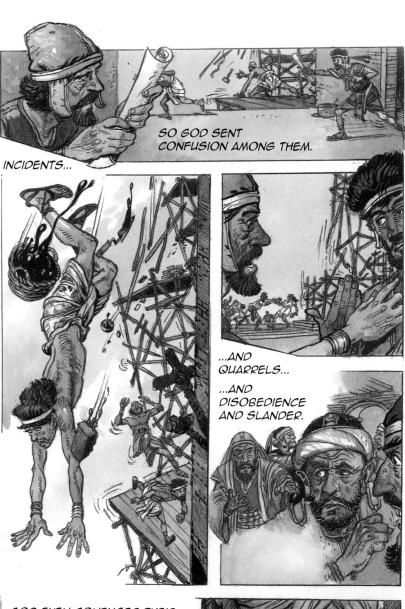

SO GOD SENT CONFUSION AMONG THEM.

INCIDENTS...

...AND QUARRELS...

...AND DISOBEDIENCE AND SLANDER.

GOD EVEN CONFUSED THEIR LANGUAGE SO THEY COULDN'T UNDERSTAND EACH OTHER, AND THEY BEGAN TO RUN AWAY. THIS WAS THE END OF THE TOWER OF BABEL. IT WAS CALLED BABEL BECAUSE GOD TURNED THEIR LANGUAGE INTO "BABBLE."

ABRAHAM'S JOURNEY OF FAITH   Genesis 12:1-20; 13,1-4

AT THE END OF THEIT LONG JOURNEY THEY PASSED THROUGH THE LAND OF THE CANAANITES AND ARRIVED AT THE OAK OF MOREH.

ABRAM, THIS IS THE PLACE I TOLD YOU ABOUT. I WILL GIVE THIS LAND TO YOU AND YOUR CHILDREN.

THERE ABRAM BUILT AN ALTAR TO GOD.

ABRAHAM CONTINUED TO EXPLORE THE LAND OF CANAAN. HE CAME TO THE HILL COUNTRY EAST OF BETHEL AND PITCHED HIS TENT THERE.

HOW WILL GOD BLESS MY CHILDREN WHEN I DON'T HAVE ANY? SARAI IS STILL NOT PREGNANT.

FROM THE HILL COUNTRY ABRAM MOVED FURTHER SOUTH TO THE NEGEV.

GOD HAS GIVEN THIS LAND TO US. WE WILL STAY HERE.

AFTERWARDS, A FAMINE CAME TO THE LAND, AND THERE WAS NOT ENOUGH FOOD FOR ABRAM'S FAMILY AND ANIMALS. THEY WERE FORCED TO GO FURTHER SOUTH TOWARDS THE LAND OF EGYPT.

SARAI, YOU'RE A BEAUTIFUL WOMAN. I'M AFRAID THE EGYPTIANS WILL WANT TO KILL ME IN ORDER TO KEEP YOU FOR THEMSELVES. TELL THEM YOU'RE MY SISTER SO THEY WON'T KILL ME.

THE KING OF EGYPT WELCOMED THE STRANGERS AND ALLOWED THEM TO SETTLE IN EGYPT DURING THE FAMINE.

THIS IS ABRAM OF HARAN AND HIS SISTER SARAI.

THE KING SAW THAT SARAI WAS EXTREMELY BEAUTIFUL, AND HE INVITED HER TO STAY WITH HIM AT THE ROYAL PALACE.

SARAI, IF YOU WILL STAY WITH ME I WILL MAKE SURE YOUR BROTHER ABRAM AND HIS SERVANTS AND HERD WILL BE WELL TAKEN CARE OF.

SOON EVERYONE IN THE PALACE GOT TERRIBLY ILL.

GOD IS PUNISHING YOU BECAUSE OF SARAI. SHE IS NOT ABRAM'S SISTER. SHE IS HIS WIFE!

OH GOD, WHAT HAVE I DONE?

WHY DID YOU LIE TO ME? SARAI IS NOT YOUR SISTER; SHE'S YOUR WIFE! GET OUT OF HERE. I NEVER WANT TO SEE YOU AGAIN.

SO ABRAM AND SARAI LEFT THE LAND OF EGYPT WITH EVERYTHING THEY OWNED, INCLUDING MANY MORE SERVANTS, CATTLE AND SHEEP.

BY NOW ABRAM WAS VERY WEALTHY AND HIS CAMELS WERE LOADED WITH SILVER AND GOLD. HIS NEPHEW LOT WAS STILL WITH HIM, AND HE WAS WEALTHY TOO. BOTH MEN HAD MANY SHEPHERDS, AND FIGHTS OFTEN BROKE OUT AMONGST THEM.

LISTEN, THIS CAN'T GO ON. OUR MEN ARE FIGHTING OVER THE PASTURES.

THE LAND CANNOT SUPPORT US ALL.

LOT, IT'S TIME WE SEPARATE. THERE'S PLENTY OF LAND, SO YOU DECIDE WHAT DIRECTION YOU WANT TO GO, AND I'LL GO THE OPPOSITE WAY.

I'LL GO EAST THEN.

GOOD, I'LL GO WEST.

SO ABRAM AND LOT PARTED. LOT WENT TOWARDS THE FERTILE PLAINS OF JORDAN. ABRAM SETTLED IN CANAAN.

ON THE PLAINS OF JORDAN WHERE LOT SETTLED, THERE WERE SEVERAL CITIES AND KINGS.

THESE KINGS WERE AT WAR WITH EACH OTHER, AND LOT AND HIS FAMILY WERE TAKEN AS PRISONERS.

YIPE!

WHEN ABRAM HEARD HIS NEPEW LOT WAS IN TROUBLE, HE MOBILIZED HIS MEN – 318 OF THEM – AND ATTACKED THE KINGS WHO HELD LOT PRISONER. ABRAM AND HIS MEN RESCUED LOT AND HIS FAMILY, INCLUDING HIS SERVANTS AND POSSESSIONS.

ABRAHAM AND LOT   Genesis 13:5-18; 14:1-24

MELCHIZEDEK, KING OF SALEM AND HIGHPRIEST OF THE MOST HIGH GOD, CAME OUT TO GREET ABRAM WITH BREAD AND WINE.

BLESSED ARE YOU, ABRAM, AND BLESSED BE GOD WHO GAVE YOU THE VICTORY OVER YOUR ENEMIES.

ABRAM GAVE MELCHIZEDEK A TENTH OF THE PLUNDER. LATER, THE KING OF SODOM WENT UP TO ABRAM.

THANK YOU FOR HELPING US OUT. I WANT YOU TO KEEP THE REST OF THE PLUNDER.

NO WAY. KEEP IT YOURSELF. I DON'T WANT YOU TO SAY THAT YOU MADE ABRAM RICH.

BACK AT THE OAK IN MAMRE, GOD SPOKE TO ABRAM IN A VISION. "KEEP TRUSTING ME," GOD SAID, "AND YOUR REWARD WILL BE GREAT."

LORD, WHAT REWARD SHALL I EXPECT? YOU PROMISED TO GIVE THIS LAND TO MY CHILDREN, BUT WHAT GOOD IS LAND IF I HAVE NO CHILDREN TO INHERIT IT?

TRUST ME, ABRAM. I WILL NOT LEAVE YOU CHILDLESS. IN DUE TIME I WILL GIVE YOU A SON AND MANY DESCENDANTS AFTER HIM.

GOD'S PROMISE TO ABRAHAM Genesis 15:1-21; 16:1-2

LOOK AT THE STARS IN THE SKY. CAN YOU COUNT THEM? THE DESCENDANTS OF YOUR CHILDREN WILL BE AS MANY AS THE STARS IN THE SKY.

GOD TOLD ABRAM TO BRING HIM SOME OF HIS ANIMALS AS A SACRIFICE. AFTER KILLING THEM ABRAM SPLIT THEM IN HALVES AND LAY THEM ON THE GROUND.

IMMEDIATELY SOME VULTURES SWOOPED DOWN ON THE DEAD ANIMALS, BUT ABRAM SCARED THEM OFF.

I TRUST YOU. BUT HOW CAN I KNOW THAT ALL THIS WILL BE MINE?

AS THE SUN WENT DOWN, A DEEP SLEEP OVERCAME ABRAM, AND HE FELT SCARED AND EXHAUSTED.

WHEN ABRAM WOKE UP, GOD SPOKE AGAIN.

AT FIRST, YOUR CHILDREN WILL LIVE AS SLAVES IN A FOREIGN LAND FOR 400 YEARS.

THEN THEY WILL MARCH OUT LOADED WITH PLUNDER. BUT BEFORE ALL THIS HAPPENS, YOU SHALL LIVE A LONG LIFE AND DIE IN PEACE.

IT WAS PITCH DARK AND ABRAM WATCHED AS A SMOKING FIRE-POT AND A FLAMING TORCH CAME DOWN AND MOVED BETWEEN THE SPLIT CARCASSES. THERE GOD RENEWED HIS COVENANT WITH ABRAM AND SAID, "I AM GIVING THIS LAND TO YOUR CHILDREN – FROM THE NILE RIVER IN EGYPT TO EUPHRATES IN ASSYRIA."

TEN YEARS WENT BY. SARAI, ABRAM'S WIFE, WAS WORRIED AS SHE REALIZED SHE WAS PROBABLY NOT ABLE TO HAVE CHILDREN. SHE WENT TO ABRAM AND SHARED WITH HIM AN IDEA SHE HAD.

LOOK, WHY DON'T YOU SLEEP WITH MY MAID HAGAR. MAYBE SHE WILL BECOME PREGNANT AND WE CAN HAVE A SON AND A FAMILY THROUGH HER.

I HOPE YOU'RE RIGHT.

HAGAR BECAME PREGNANT AND SHE BEGAN TO DESPISE HER MISTRESS SARAI.
SARAI FELT HURT AND JEALOUS.

LOOK AT HAGAR. CAN'T YOU SEE HOW BAD SHE'S TREATING ME? THIS ISN'T FAIR. DO SOMETHING.

SHE'S YOUR MAID. YOU DEAL WITH IT.

SO SARAI MISTREATED HER MAID HAGAR.

AIYEEEE!

FINALLY HAGAR RAN AWAY.

I'M NOT GOING TO TAKE THIS ABUSE ANYMORE. I'D RATHER DIE IN THE DESERT.

THE ANGEL OF GOD FOUND HAGAR AT A SPRING IN THE DESERT.

HAGAR, WHAT ARE YOU DOING OUT HERE?

I'M RUNNING AWAY FROM MY MISTRESS.

THE ANGEL TOLD HAGAR TO GO BACK. HE ALSO PROMISED HER A SON AND MANY DESCENDANTS AFTER HIM. "YOUR SON SHALL BE CALLED ISHMAEL," HE TOLD HER

I'M BACK.

HAGAR GAVE BIRTH TO A SON, JUST LIKE THE ANGEL SAID. ABRAM CALLED HIS SON ISHMAEL. ABRAM WAS 86 YEARS OLD WHEN ISHMAEL WAS BORN.

HAGAR AND SARAH   Genesis 16:3-16; 17:1-27; 18:1-15

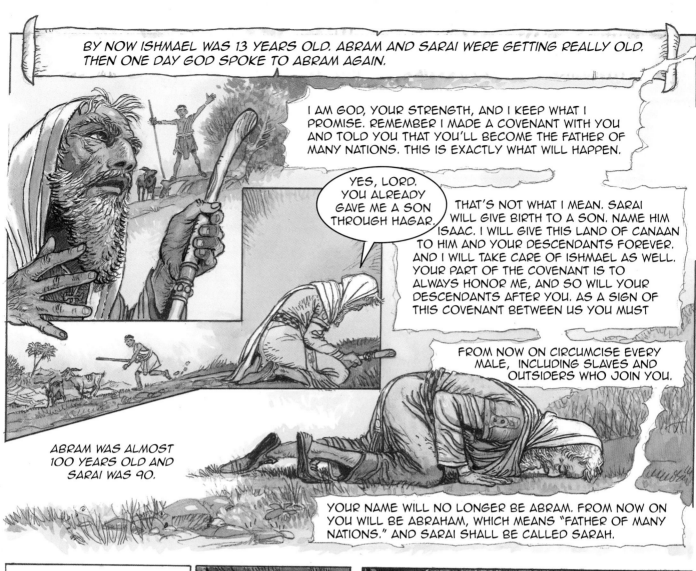

BY NOW ISHMAEL WAS 13 YEARS OLD. ABRAM AND SARAI WERE GETTING REALLY OLD. THEN ONE DAY GOD SPOKE TO ABRAM AGAIN.

I AM GOD, YOUR STRENGTH, AND I KEEP WHAT I PROMISE. REMEMBER I MADE A COVENANT WITH YOU AND TOLD YOU THAT YOU'LL BECOME THE FATHER OF MANY NATIONS. THIS IS EXACTLY WHAT WILL HAPPEN.

YES, LORD. YOU ALREADY GAVE ME A SON THROUGH HAGAR.

THAT'S NOT WHAT I MEAN. SARAI WILL GIVE BIRTH TO A SON. NAME HIM ISAAC. I WILL GIVE THIS LAND OF CANAAN TO HIM AND YOUR DESCENDANTS FOREVER. AND I WILL TAKE CARE OF ISHMAEL AS WELL. YOUR PART OF THE COVENANT IS TO ALWAYS HONOR ME, AND SO WILL YOUR DESCENDANTS AFTER YOU. AS A SIGN OF THIS COVENANT BETWEEN US YOU MUST

FROM NOW ON CIRCUMCISE EVERY MALE, INCLUDING SLAVES AND OUTSIDERS WHO JOIN YOU.

ABRAM WAS ALMOST 100 YEARS OLD AND SARAI WAS 90.

YOUR NAME WILL NO LONGER BE ABRAM. FROM NOW ON YOU WILL BE ABRAHAM, WHICH MEANS "FATHER OF MANY NATIONS." AND SARAI SHALL BE CALLED SARAH.

THREE MONTHS LATER, AT THE GREAT OAK OF MAMRE.

HELLO, STRANGERS.

PLEASE, COME AND REST FOR A WHILE AND I'LL PROVIDE FRESH WATER AND FOOD FOR YOU.

THANK YOU.

QUICK, SARAH, BAKE SOME BREAD WHILE I GO AND SLAUGHTER OUR BEST CALF. THE MEN NEED SOMETHING TO EAT.

C'MON, HURRY UP, BULLIE.

HERE'S SOME FRESH BREAD.

THANKS, THAT'S GREAT.

THIS WILL REFRESH THEM.

WHERE IS SARAH, YOUR WIFE?

INSIDE THE TENT, SIR.

I'LL COME BACK ABOUT THIS TIME NEXT YEAR. WHEN I DO, SARAH WILL HAVE GIVEN BIRTH TO A SON.

ME, AN OLD WOMAN? HA, THAT'S VERY FUNNY.

WHY DID SARAH LAUGH? IS ANYTHING TOO HARD FOR GOD? I SAID, NEXT YEAR SARAH WILL HAVE A SON.

I DIDN'T LAUGH.

YES, YOU DID.

26

THE THREE MEN THANKED ABRAHAM FOR HIS HOSPITALITY. ABRAHAM SAW THEM OUT.

WHERE ARE YOU HEADING?

WE'RE GOING TO THE CITY OF SODOM.

WHY SODOM?

LISTEN, ABRAHAM, GOD HAS CHOSEN TO BLESS YOU AND YOUR DESCENDANTS FOR-EVER IF YOU LIVE KINDLY AND FAIRLY BEFORE HIM.

BUT THE SINS OF SODOM AND GOMORRAH ARE TOO MANY. I HEAR THE CRIES OF THE INNOCENT PEOPLE IN THOSE CITIES, AND NOW I WILL GO THERE TO SEE FOR MYSELF WHAT IT'S LIKE.

THE MEN SET OUT FOR SODOM BUT ABRAHAM BLOCKED THEIR WAY.

HEY, WAIT UP!

ARE YOU SERIOUS? ARE YOU REALLY GOING TO DESTROY THE GOOD PEOPLE WITH THE BAD?

WHAT IF THERE ARE 50 GOOD PEOPLE? HOW CAN GOD BE SO UNFAIR?

OK, I'LL SPARE THE CITY IF I FIND 50 GOOD PEOPLE THERE.

WHAT IF THEY FALL SHORT OF ONLY 5?

OK, I'LL STILL SPARE THEM.

WHAT IF THERE ARE ONLY 40?

YES, I'LL SPARE THEM.

30?

YES.

20?

ABRAHAM TOOK COURAGE AND ASKED ONE LAST TIME.

PLEASE, MASTER, DON'T BE ANGRY WITH ME. WHAT IF THERE ARE ONLY 10 GOOD PEOPLE? WILL YOU STILL SPARE THE CITY FOR THEIR SAKE?

YES, ABRAHAM, I'LL SPARE THEM.

GOD LISTENED TO ABRAHAM BECAUSE GOD CONSIDERED HIM HIS FRIEND. FINALLY GOD LEFT AND ABRAHAM WENT HOME TO SARAH.

27   **SODOM AND GOMORRAH**   Genesis 18:16-33; 19:1-38

THE TWO ANGELS ARRIVED IN SODOM WHERE LOT WAS WAITING AT THE CITY GATE. HE WELCOMED THEM AND INVITED THEM TO HIS HOUSE. THEY SAID THEY PREFERRED TO SLEEP IN THE STREET, BUT LOT INSISTED. HE DIDN'T WANT THEM TO SEE THE PEOPLE PARTYING IN THE STREET.

DURING THE NIGHT SOME EVIL MEN CAME TO LOT'S HOUSE.

THE TWO MEN REACHED OUT AND QUICKLY PULLED LOT INSIDE.

THEN THEY STRUCK BLIND THE EVIL MEN OUTSIDE.

THE NEXT MORNING ABRAHAM WENT UP AND SAW THE SMOKE THAT ROSE FROM THE LOST CITIES OF SODOM AND GOMORRAH.

GOD DIDN'T SPARE THE CITIES BUT HE RESCUED LOT AND HIS TWO DAUGHTERS. THEY SETTLED IN A CAVE IN THE MOUNTAINS ABOVE THE PLAINS OF JORDAN.

LOT'S DAUGHTERS GOT PREGNANT AND GAVE BIRTH TO TWO SONS – MOAB, THE ANCESTOR OF THE MOABITES; AND BEN-AMMI, THE ANCESTOR OF THE AMMONITES.

ABRAHAM TRAVELED SOUTH AND SETTLED DOWN BETWEEN KADESH AND SHUR. GOD BLESSED HIM AND ABRAHAM WAS NOW A WEALTHY MAN.

GOD KEPT HIS PROMISE TO SARAH AND ABRAHAM. DESPITE THEIR OLD AGE, SARAH FINALLY BECAME PREGNANT AND GAVE BIRTH TO A SON.

MY SON, YOU WILL BE CALLED ISAAC, WHICH MEANS "LAUGHTER."

YES, GOD HAS BLESSED ME WITH LAUGHTER. ALL WHO HEAR ABOUT THIS WILL SURELY LAUGH OUT LOUD WITH ME.

ABRAHAM FELT BAD ABOUT IT BUT HE DIDN'T KNOW WHAT TO DO. AFTER ALL BOTH BOYS WERE HIS SONS.

TWO YEARS WENT BY. ISAAC WAS NOW A TODDLER AND HIS HALF-BROTHER ISHMAEL WAS A BIG BOY. SARAH NOTICED THAT ISHMAEL WAS SOMETIMES POKING FUN AT ISAAC.

DON'T YOU SEE WHAT'S GOING ON? WE MUST GET RID OF THIS SLAVE GIRL AND HER SON.

GOD SPOKE TO ABRAHAM AND TOLD HIM TO DO WHAT SARAH DEMANDED.

MY PROMISE TO YOU WILL BE FULFILLED THROUGH YOUR SON ISAAC. BUT DON'T WORRY. I WILL GREATLY BLESS YOUR OTHER SON TOO.

ISAAC, SON OF PROMISE   Genesis 21:1-34

In the meantime Abraham settled in Beersheba where the Philistines lived. He dug a well so he could draw water for his animals. But some servants of the Philistine King Abimelech took possession of the well, and Abraham confronted the king. Abimelech realized God was with Abraham so he quickly made an agreement with Abraham that secured Abraham the well and some land around it.

ISAAC WAS ABOUT 13 WHEN GOD SPOKE TO ABRAHAM AGAIN.

ABRAHAM!

LORD. I'M LISTENING.

I KNOW YOU LOVE YOUR SON ISAAC VERY MUCH. THEREFORE, I WANT YOU TO TAKE HIM TO THE LAND OF MORIAH.

BUT WHY, LORD?

I WILL POINT OUT A PLACE IN MORIAH. THERE I WANT YOU TO SACRIFICE ISAAC AS A BURNT OFFERING TO ME.

I DON'T QUITE FOLLOW YOU, LORD.

GOD'S ONLY ANSWER WAS SILENCE. IT SLOWLY DAWNED ON ABRAHAM WHAT GOD WAS ASKING OF HIM. HE WAS ASKING HIM TO KILL HIS OWN SON SO GOD WOULD BE PLEASED.

THIS IS FOR YOUR OWN GOOD. YOU WILL NEED TO LET GO OF YOUR SON.

ARGH

GOD, HOW CAN YOU DO THIS TO ME?

THAT NIGHT ABRAHAM TOOK A LONG LAST LOOK AT HIS BELOVED SON. HADN'T GOD PROMISED TO GIVE HIM MANY DESCENDANTS THROUGH HIM? HOW COME HE NOW WANTED HIM TO DIE? HAD GOD CHANGED HIS MIND?

EARLY THE NEXT MORNING, ABRAHAM SADDLED A DONKEY AND LOADED FIREWOOD ONTO IT. ALSO HE TOLD TWO OF HIS FAITHFUL SERVANTS TO GET READY FOR THE JOURNEY.

YES, SON, YOU MAY COME WITH ME.

DAD, MAY I GO WITH YOU?

THE SACRIFICE OF ISAAC Genesis 22:1-19

ABRAHAM AND ISAAC RETURNED TO THE SERVANTS WHO WERE WAITING BELOW THE MOUNTAIN. AGAIN GOD'S ANGEL SPOKE TO ABRAHAM.

MY DEAR SON ABRAHAM, BECAUSE YOU WERE OBEDIENT AND WILLING TO GIVE UP YOUR OWN SON, YOUR DESCENDANTS THROUGH ISAAC SHALL BE AS MANY AS THE STARS IN THE SKY AND THE SAND ON THE BEACH. AND I WILL GREATLY BLESS THEM.

ISAAC HAS CERTAINLY BROUGHT US LAUGHTER.

YEARS WENT BY. ISAAC WAS NOW A YOUNG MAN, AND HE BROUGHT GREAT JOY TO HIS PARENTS SARAH AND ABRAHAM IN THEIR OLD AGE.

SARAH WAS 127 YEARS OLD WHEN SHE DIED. ABRAHAM MOURNED HIS DEAR WIFE AND BOUGHT LAND FOR A BURIAL SITE FROM THE CHIEF OF THE HITTITES AND BURIED SARAH IN A CAVE NEAR MAMRE IN PRESENT-DAY HEBRON.

I'M AN OLD MAN AND SOON I SHALL DIE TOO. BEFORE I DIE I MUST FIND A PROPER WIFE FOR ISAAC SO GOD'S PROMISES CAN BE FULFILLED.

ABRAHAM CALLED HIS FAITHFUL SERVANT ELIEZER AND TOLD HIM TO GO BACK TO ABRAHAM'S HOMELAND.

I WANT YOU TO FIND A WIFE FOR ISAAC AMONG MY OWN PEOPLE.

VERY WELL, SIR, BUT WHAT SHOULD I DO IF THIS WOMAN REFUSES TO LEAVE HER PEOPLE AND GO BACK WITH ME?

SHALL I THEN BRING ISAAC TO HER?

NEVER EVER. THIS IS THE LAND GOD HAS PROMISED HIM. ISAAC BELONGS HERE.

GOD WILL SEND HIS ANGEL AHEAD OF YOU. HE WILL FIND THE RIGHT WIFE FOR ISAAC.

ELIEZER LOADED TEN CAMELS WITH GIFTS AND SET OUT FOR HARAN IN THE EAST.

AFTER MANY DAYS ELIEZER ARRIVED AT THE CITY OF HARAN.

ISAAC AND REBEKAH Genesis 24:1-67; 25:1-11

GOD OF ABRAHAM, HELP ME FIND THE RIGHT GIRL. I TRUST THAT THE ONE WHO IS MOST KIND TO ME AND OFFERS MY CAMELS A DRINK WILL BE THE ONE.

HELLO, STRANGER.

HELLO, WE HAVE COME A LONG WAY AND ARE TIRED AND THIRSTY. MAY I HAVE A DRINK FROM YOUR JUG?

CERTAINLY, SIR. PLEASE ALLOW ME TO ALSO DRAW WATER FOR YOUR CAMELS.

THANK YOU. PLEASE TAKE THIS GIFT FOR YOUR KINDNESS. WHAT'S YOUR NAME?

I'M REBEKAH, THE DAUGHTER OF BETHUEL. YOU MAY STAY AT MY FATHER'S HOUSE FOR THE NIGHT.

WHEN ELIEZER REALIZED THAT BETHUEL, REBEKAH'S FATHER, WAS A BROTHER OF ABRAHAM, HE WAS POSITIVE REBEKAH WAS THE RIGHT GIRL FOR ISAAC. ELIEZER KNELT AT THE WELL TO WORSHIP WHILE REBEKAH RAN HOME AND TOLD HER BROTHER LABAN WHAT HAD HAPPENED. LABAN CAME OUT TO GREET ELIEZER.

ELIEZER FOLLOWED LABAN TO BETHUEL'S HOUSE WHERE HE WAS WELL TAKEN CARE OF. HE TOLD THEM HOW HIS MASTER HAD SENT HIM OUT TO FIND A WIFE FOR ISAAC AND HOW HE HAD MET REBEKAH AT THE WELL.

HOW CAN I THEN SAY NO? REBEKAH HAS ANSWERED FOR HERSELF. THIS IS NOT FOR ME TO DECIDE. THIS IS TOTALLY FROM GOD. MAY HE BLESS YOU, MY DAUGHTER!!

THANK YOU, LORD, FOR LEADING ME RIGHT TO THE DOOR OF MY MASTER'S BROTHER.

PLEASE COME TO OUR HOUSE AND BE OUR GUEST. WE HAVE ROOM FOR YOU AND YOUR CAMELS.

WILL YOU ALLOW ME TO TAKE REBEKAH WITH ME BACK TO MY MASTER'S SON?

WHAT DO *YOU* SAY, REBEKAH?

I WILL. I'M READY.

ISAAC WAS OUT IN THE FIELD WHEN HE LOOKED UP AND SAW THE CARAVAN COMING.

WHO CAN THIS BE?

AS ISAAC CAME CLOSER, REBEKAH GOT DOWN FROM HER CAMEL AND QUICKLY COVERED HER FACE.

WHO'S THIS, ELIEZER?

THIS IS ISAAC, MY MASTER.

HELLO.

ELIEZER TOLD ISAAC THE WHOLE STORY OF HOW HE HAD FOUND REBEKAH. ISAAC SAW HOW BEAUTIFUL SHE WAS, AND HE FELL IN LOVE WITH HER.

WELCOME, REBEKAH.

THIS IS GOD'S DOING.

ISAAC TOOK REBEKAH INTO THE TENT OF HIS MOTHER SARAH AND MARRIED HER RIGHT THERE

ISAAC LOVED REBEKAH AND SHE GAVE HIM COMFORT AFTER THE LOSS OF HIS MOTHER. SOON AFTER, ABRAHAM DIED TOO – HAPPY AT A RIPE OLD AGE AND FULL OF YEARS. HE WAS BURIED NEXT TO SARAH AT THE BURIAL SITE HE HAD BOUGHT FROM THE HITTITE CHIEF NEAR MAMRE. ABRAHAM LEFT ALL HIS RICHES TO ISAAC, AND GOD BLESSED ISAAC AND REBEKAH VERY MUCH.

TWENTY YEARS WENT BY AND ISAAC AND REBEKAH WERE STILL CHILDLESS. ISAAC WAS GETTING WORRIED.

GOD OF MY FATHER ABRAHAM, I THANK YOU FOR THIS LAND YOU HAVE GIVEN ME WHERE WE CAN LIVE AT PEACE WITH OUR NEIGHBORS,

BUT MY WIFE IS BARREN. WHAT GOOD IS LAND WHEN I DON'T HAVE A SON TO INHERIT IT?

GOD HEARD ISAAC'S PRAYERS AND REBEKAH BECAME PREGNANT.

LOOK! THE BABY IS KICKING.

BUT REBEKAH CARRIED MORE THAN ONE BABY. SOON SHE REALIZED THERE WERE TWO BABIES KICKING IN HER WOMB.

OH GOD, THIS IS UNBEARABLE. IT FEELS LIKE THE BABIES ARE FIGHTING INSIDE ME. GOD, WHAT'S GOING ON?

SOB!

TWO NATIONS ARE BUTTING HEADS INSIDE YOU. THE OLDER SHALL SERVE THE YOUNGER.

AAAAH!

FINALLY REBEKAH GAVE BIRTH TO TWO SONS, ESAU AND JACOB.

THE BOYS WERE QUITE DIFFERENT. JACOB WAS A QUIET BOY WHO LIKED TO HELP HIS MOTHER AROUND THE TENT. REBEKAH LOVED JACOB.

IS THIS GOOD, MOM?

SHAKE IT A LITTLE MORE. THAT'LL BE PERFECT.

ESAU PREFERED THE OUTDOORS. HE BECAME A GREAT HUNTER. ISAAC LOVED ESAU.

JACOB AND ESAU Genesis 25:21-34; 27:1-46

ONE DAY ESAU WAS OUT HUNTING.

ZOOM!

TIME AFTER TIME THE GAME ESCAPED HIS ARROWS.

ARG! MISSED AGAIN!

ZOOM!

AT THE END OF THE DAY ESAU WAS VERY TIRED AND HUNGRY. HE DECIDED TO GO HOME.

AH, WHAT'S THAT? I SMELL SOMETHING. IT SMELLS WONDERFUL.

BACK AT THE TENT, JACOB WAS COOKING A MEAL FOR HIMSELF.

HEY BROTHER, WHAT'S COOKING? CAN I HAVE SOME OF THAT WONDERFUL RED STEW? I'M STARVING!

OK. YOU GET MY STEW IF YOU GIVE ME YOUR RIGHTS AS THE FIRSTBORN.

ALRIGHT. THAT'S A DEAL.

JACOB WAS PLAYING A CUNNING TRICK ON HIS OLDER BROTHER.

THEN SWEAR TO ME.

ESAU SWORE THAT HE WOULD GIVE UP HIS RIGHTS AND THREW HIMSELF ON THE FOOD.

SSSLURP!

HA, NOW I'M THE RIGHTFUL HEIR TO OUR FATHER'S WEALTH AND NAME.

SSSLURP!

EVENTUALLY ESAU REALIZED HOW STUPID HE HAD BEEN IN SHRUGGING OFF HIS RIGHTS FOR A DISH OF LENTILS. HE DIDN'T WANT HIS FATHER TO KNOW ABOUT IT SO HE DECIDED NOT TO TELL HIM. JACOB, HOWEVER, TOLD HIS MOTHER ALL ABOUT IT.

GOD BLESSED ISAAC, AND HIS WEALTH INCREASED. HE HAD MANY HERDS, FLOCKS AND SERVANTS. HE LIVED IN PEACE WITH THE NEIGHBORING TRIBES, AND THEY LOOKED UP TO HIM BECAUSE THEY COULD SEE HOW BLESSED HE WAS. BY NOW HE WAS VERY OLD AND NEARLY BLIND. BEFORE HE DIED HE WANTED TO BLESS ESAU, HIS FIRSTBORN.

ESAU, MY FIRSTBORN, GOD HAS GIVEN YOU ALL THIS LAND THROUGH YOUR GRANDFATHER ABRAHAM.

IT'S ALL YOURS AFTER I'VE BLESSED YOU.

BUT FATHER, CAN'T YOU ALSO BLESS ME LIKE YOU BLESSED JACOB?

NO, THAT'S IMPOSSIBLE. JACOB GOT IT ALL. HE WILL FOREVER BE THE MASTER OF HIS BROTHERS.

YOU'LL HAVE TO SERVE YOUR BROTHER AND LIVE BY YOUR SWORD. BUT WHEN YOU'RE FED UP YOU'LL FINALLY BREAK FREE.

REBEKAH SENSED THAT ESAU WAS GOING TO TAKE REVENGE AND KILL JACOB. SHE REALIZED JACOB'S LIFE WAS IN DANGER. SHE THOUGHT ABOUT IT AND CAME UP WITH A PLAN...

SHE REMEMBERED HER BROTHER LABAN BACK AT HARAN. JACOB WOULD BE SAFE WITH HIM. BUT HOW COULD SHE CONVINCE ISAAC IT WAS A GOOD IDEA TO SEND JACOB AWAY?

FRANKLY SPEAKING, ISAAC, I'M SICK OF THE LOCAL WOMEN ESAU HAS MARRIED.

I DON'T WANT JACOB TO MAKE THE SAME MISTAKE.

RIGHT.

SOUNDS GOOD TO ME. I'LL TALK TO HIM.

HERE'S WHAT WE'LL DO. WE'LL SEND JACOB AWAY TO LABAN IN HARAN.

JACOB, I WANT YOU TO GO AWAY FOR A WHILE UNTIL YOUR BROTHER HAS COOLED OFF.

GO TO YOUR UNCLE IN HARAN AND LIVE THERE. WHEN YOU'RE READY TO MARRY, PICK A GIRL AMONG LABAN'S DAUGHTERS.

AND MAY GOD BLESS YOU AND GIVE YOU MANY CHILDREN IN THIS LAND GOD PROMISED YOUR GRANDFATHER ABRAHAM.

JACOB OBEYED ISAAC AND REBEKAH. THAT NIGHT HE LEFT BEERSHEBA AND SET OUT FOR FAR-AWAY HARAN.

THIS WAS A LONG AND TIRING JOURNEY, AND JACOB WAS NOT USED TO THE WILDERNESS LIKE HIS BROTHER ESAU. HE HARDLY KNEW HOW TO DEFEND HIM- SELF AGAINST THE WILD ANIMALS.

DURING THE NIGHTS, HE SOMETIMES FOUND SHELTER IN SPOOKY PLACES.

GOD, I'M SO SCARED. PLEASE HELP ME.

DURING THE DAY, HE WAS OVER- WHELMED BY WORRY AND FATIGUE.

I DON'T THINK I CAN MAKE IT ANY LONGER.

THAT VERY NIGHT JACOB HAD A VIVID DREAM. IN HIS DREAM HE SAW A STAIR- CASE CONNECTING HEAVEN AND EARTH, AND ANGELS OF GOD WERE COMING DOWN THE STAIRS AND GOING BACK UP AGAIN. THEN HE HEARD THE VOICE OF GOD...

I WONDER IF MY FATHER DROVE ME INTO THIS WASTE- LAND TO PUNISH ME BECAUSE I STOLE ESAU'S BIRTHRIGHT.

ONE NIGHT HE COLLAPSED AND LAY DOWN ON A STONE TO SLEEP.

I'M THE GOD OF ABRAHAM. I AM FAITHFUL TO THE PROMISES I GAVE HIM. THIS VERY PLACE WILL BE YOURS, AND YOUR DESCENDANTS WILL SPREAD LIKE DUST FROM WEST TO EAST AND FROM NORTH TO SOUTH. IN FACT, ALL THE PEOPLES OF THE EARTH SHALL BE BLESSED THROUGH YOU. DON'T WORRY. I AM GOD, AND I AM WITH YOU.

WHAT? GOD IS CERTAINLY IN THIS PLACE, AND I WASN'T EVEN AWARE OF IT.

THIS IS SCARY -- A HOLY PLACE, THE HOUSE OF GOD, THE GATE OF HEAVEN!

JACOB FINALLY WENT BACK TO SLEEP.

THE NEXT MORNING HE WOKE UP REFRESHED AND ENCOURAGED.

THIS STONE I SLEPT ON WILL BE A MEMORIAL PILLAR.

THIS WILL BE FOR ALL TO SEE THAT HEAVEN AND EARTH ARE ONE.

THEN HE POURED OIL ON THE ALTAR AND CHRISTENED THE PLACE.

THIS WILL BE CALLED BETHEL, THE HOUSE OF GOD.

JACOB CONTINUED HIS LONELY JOURNEY, BUT NOW HE FELT LIGHT IN HIS HEART, AS WELL AS, IN HIS FEET.

GOD HAS GIVEN ME COURAGE. HE WILL BE MY GOD. HE WILL PROTECT ME AND BRING ME BACK SAFELY TO MY FATHER'S HOUSE.

HE FINALLY ARRIVED AT HARAN. OUTSIDE THE TOWN WAS A WELL WITH SHEEP AND SHEPHERDS ALL AROUND.

HELLO, FRIENDS, WOULD YOU HAP-PEN TO KNOW A MAN CALLED LABAN, SON OF NAHOR?

OF COURSE. EVERYONE KNOWS LABAN. HE LIVES HERE. HIS DAUGHTER RACHEL IS JUST COMING OVER THERE WITH HER FLOCK.